the cloning controversy

Sean McCollum

Steck Vaughn™

A Harcourt Achieve Imprint

www.Steck-Vaughn.com
1-800-531-5015

The Cloning Controversy
By Sean McCollum

Photo Acknowledgements

Cover [TK]; p. 3 ©L.Willatt/East Anglian Regional Genetics Service/Photo Researchers, Inc.; p. 5c ©Mark Smith/Photo Researchers, Inc.; p. 5b www.glofish.com; p. 7 ©Johner/ Johner Images/Getty Images; p. 9 U.S Department of Energy Human Genome Program; p. 12–13 ©Reuters/CORBIS; p. 15 ©The Roslin Institute; p. 18–19 ©W. Perry Conway/ CORBIS; p. 23 ©20th Century Fox/The Kobal Collection; p. 27 ©L.Willatt/East Anglian Regional Genetics Service/Photo Researchers, Inc.; p. 29 ©Jade Albert Studio, Inc./Taxi/Getty Images.

Additional photography by Photodisc/Getty Royalty Free, and Royalty-Free/CORBIS.

Illustration Acknowledgements

p. 17 Jane Whitney; p. 25 Jane Whitney

ISBN-13: 978-1-4190-2301-9
ISBN-10:   1-4190-2301-2

Printed in China

1 2 3 4 5 6 7 8 788 13 12 11 10 09 08 07 06

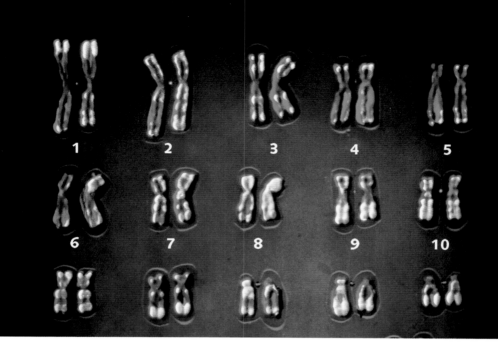

Table of Contents

Introduction

A Brave New World

What do you get when you cross a jellyfish with a zebrafish? It sounds like a joke. It's not. The result is a pet fish that glows in the dark.

How is this possible? Jellyfish and zebrafish don't mate in nature. You might as well try to cross a spider with a goat. Don't laugh. Scientists can do this now, too, by mixing the animals' **genes**.

Genes are special chemical codes. Every living thing has a unique set of genes that controls how it looks and grows. That includes you. Each of your parents gave you one-half of your genes.

Fifty years ago, we knew very little about genes. Today, genetic scientists are trying to figure out what each gene controls. They hope to find and fix genes that cause disease. Scientists can already use genes to make **clones**, or exact copies, of animals. Should we **modify** nature's most basic plan for life? Read on and decide.

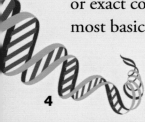

The jellyfish on top glows. When it's crossed with a zebrafish, you get a fish that glows in the dark.

Chapter 1

SPIDER-GOATS AND BUG-KILLING CORN

Move over, Spider-Man™. Ordinary humans may soon be using the incredible power of spider webs. For its weight, spider silk is stronger than anything on Earth. A rope of spider-silk as thick as your thumb would be strong enough to lift a jumbo jet. A light vest of spider threads could stop a bullet.

Stealing a spider's powers is no simple task. In nature, spiders don't make enough silk for humans to harvest. Raising groups of spiders won't work either. They would eat each other.

Genetics may soon solve this problem. Scientists have found the spider gene that creates silk. A Canadian company discovered how to give the gene to a goat. First, they take the gene from a kind of spider called an orb weaver. Then, they put it into a goat embryo, or fertilized egg. The embryo grows inside a female goat. The female gives birth to baby goats with spider genes. When they grow up, they produce spider silk **proteins** in their milk. Machines filter the milk and spin out spider silk.

No one is towing jets with spider-silk ropes—yet. The process is still too expensive.

Changing a plant or animal's DNA is called **genetic** engineering. The spider-goat is only one example. The products of genetic engineering are called GMOs, or genetically modified **organisms**. Farmers use the process to create tougher, more nutritious crops. Genetic engineers may soon produce GMO foods that contain medicine. We can't even imagine all the possibilities.

That fact scares some people. Genetic experiments could produce odd-looking or dangerous creatures. Will scientists upset some kind of natural balance? For now, no one knows the answers.

"Spider-goats" have 70,000 goat genes and just one from a spider. That one spider gene makes a big difference in their milk.

Blueprint for Life

To understand genetics, you must think small. Every living thing is made of **cells**. Most cells can only be seen through a microscope. Your body is made of about 100 trillion of them.

Cells are like tiny factories. Inside each cell is a **nucleus**. The nucleus acts as the control room for the factory. In that control room are your genes. Genes tell each cell how to grow and what to do.

All the genes of an organism are called its **genome** (JEE-nome). Your genome is your **microscopic** building plan. It exists in almost every cell of your body except your red blood cells. The genome determines how tall you are. It decides whether you have black hair or green eyes.

Where did your genome come from? Half of it came from your mother and half came from your father. The two halves combined to form one **unique** set—*you*.

Your genome is different from every other person's genome—unless you have an identical twin. Identical twins have the exact same gene pattern.

A human genome contains 23 pairs of **chromosomes**. Chromosomes are made of DNA (deoxyribonucleic acid).

In a microscope, DNA looks like a twisted rope ladder. The "steps" of the ladder are made of four chemicals: adenine (A), thymine (T), cytosine (C), and guanine (G). The four chemicals always pair up the same way. A pairs with T, and C pairs with G. A human genome has three billion of these pairs. In each organism,

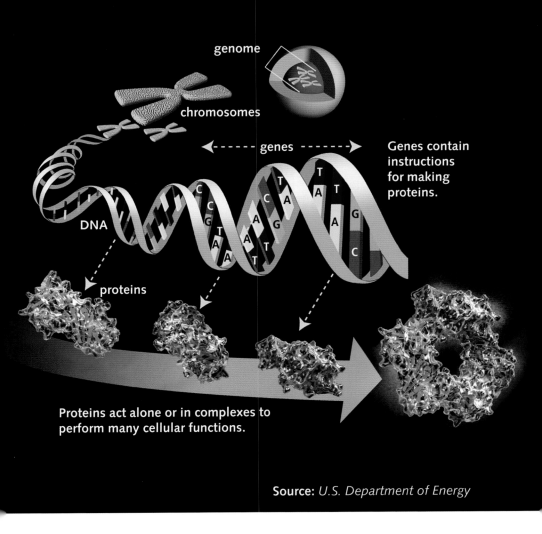

genome

chromosomes

genes

DNA

Genes contain instructions for making proteins.

proteins

Proteins act alone or in complexes to perform many cellular functions.

Source: *U.S. Department of Energy*

they line up in a unique order. That's the gene code. Only two percent of the genome contains code. No one knows what the rest of the DNA does!

Gene base pairs tell cells to produce proteins. One molecule of DNA can hold the plans for thousands of different proteins. Protein is the building block for making more of you.

Stirring the Gene Pool

Humans have been **tinkering** with genes for hundreds of years. The process is called *selective breeding*. The difference between a Rottweiler and a poodle is an example. In fact, all pure breeds have been created by selective breeding for different **traits.** Plants can be selectively bred as well. Gardeners can control the **pollination** of roses to create new colors.

Genetic engineering uses a much more complex process. The process is called *transgenics*. That's how the Canadian company produced spider silk from goat's milk.

Scientists can also **alter** the genes in a single organism. That's how they made the "Flavr Savr™" tomato. This was the first GMO sold commercially.

The Flavr Savr™ solved a big problem for tomato growers. Tomatoes often rot on the way to the store. To keep them from rotting, farmers pick them while they're green. Green tomatoes don't rot during shipping. They also don't taste very good.

Scientists wanted to create a tomato that rots slowly. They identified the gene that causes tomatoes to rot. Then, they created a reverse copy of the gene. They inserted the reverse copy into a tomato seed. Farmers could let the Flavr Savr™ ripen on the vine. It stayed perfectly fresh all the way to the dinner table.

Genetic engineering can also help plants fight off pests. In one kind of corn, a new gene creates a **pesticide**. This poison kills corn borer bugs. That means a bigger harvest for farmers.

Scientists are experimenting with bananas. They are trying to make a genetic change that would cause the bananas to produce a **vaccine**. Vaccines help make people **immune** to diseases. Imagine getting a banana instead of a shot! Another change could create bananas that are supercharged with vitamins. Farmers already grow genetically modified "golden rice." Golden rice has large amounts of vitamin A. Vitamin-packed food would help people across the globe.

Some people worry about the effects of genetically modified foods. Others say it only improves the quality of what we eat.

11

More Harm Than Good?

The benefits of GMOs are obvious. The drawbacks are harder to see. Consider the genetically modified bananas. The vaccine might help humans, but what about birds and other wild animals that might eat them? Genetically modified corn allows farmers to use less pesticide. Yet, the corn itself is producing a poison. It could kill more than just corn borer bugs.

Some people worry about the long-term effects of GMOs. Jeremy Rifkin heads the Foundation of Economic Trends. "Remember, genetically modified products are alive," says Rifkin. That makes it hard to predict what they'll do.

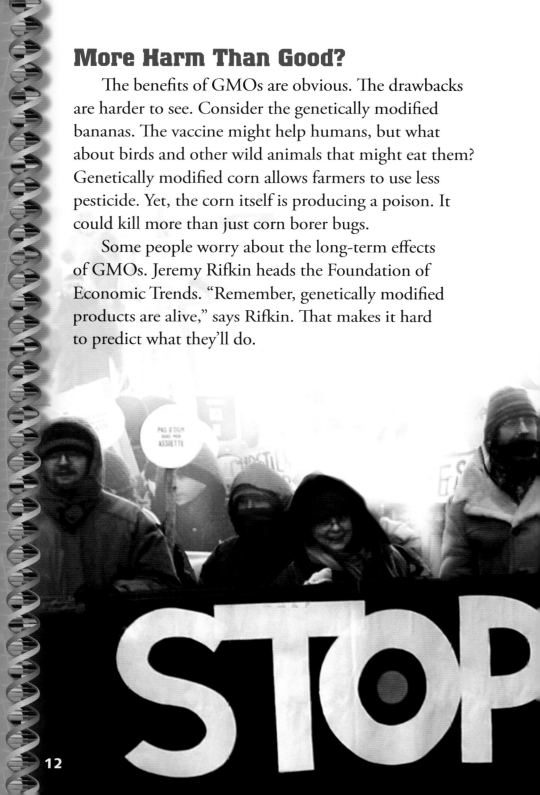

In Great Britain, for example, scientists modified a crop to withstand a weed killer. Farmers could then spray their fields with poisons. The poisons would kill weeds but leave the crop unharmed. The poison-fighting gene, however, was transferred to the weeds. That made them harder to kill, too. Will GMOs do more harm than good? The answer isn't clear. Yet, GMOs are already here. We've already started changing the blueprint of life—for better or worse.

Demonstrators march in the streets of Montreal, Canada, during a protest against GMOs.

Chapter 2

CARBON COPIES: CLONING AT WORK

For decades, many scientists thought cloning was impossible. Take a grown animal and make an exact copy—no scientists could do that, could they? It sounded like science fiction.

Then, in February 1997, the world met Dolly. She didn't look like a major scientific **breakthrough**. She looked like a cute little lamb.

This cute little lamb, however, did not get her genes from a mother sheep and a father sheep. She got all of her genes from a single cell of an adult sheep. Dolly was an exact copy of that adult sheep. How did it happen? See the chart on page 16. She was the world's first truly cloned **mammal**.

Within weeks, Dolly became the most famous sheep ever born. Her picture appeared everywhere. She amazed people. However, Dolly's birth raised a lot of questions. Could a clone live a healthy life? Would we start cloning animals for milk and meat? Would that make us sick? Had science gone too far? Could cloning humans be far behind? Were scientists going too far?

Dolly's death in 2003 raised even more questions. She died of lung disease at the age of six. Sheep can live twice as long as that. And lung disease usually affects older sheep. Was cloning to blame? If so, should we stop experimenting?

Dolly was created from a single cell of a Finn Dorset sheep. The resulting embryo was implanted in a Scottish Blackface sheep. She was an exact copy of the Finn Dorset donor.

Dolly broke all the rules. She was created from a single parent's genes. The team in Scotland tried 277 times. Finally, they succeeded.

1. An egg was taken from a female Blackface sheep. Scientists got rid of the DNA in the egg.

2. Then, they took a cell from a female white-faced Finn Dorset sheep.

3. The Finn Dorset cell was placed beside the empty egg, then an electric current was used to fuse them. The shock bonded the Finn Dorset DNA with the Blackface egg.

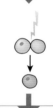

4. The cell in the new egg divided and turned into an embryonic sheep. Scientists implanted the embryo in the womb of a different Blackface sheep.

5. Dolly was born with all of the traits of a white-faced Finn Dorset sheep.

Natural Clones

Cloning seems like space-age science. Yet, clones are common in nature. Identical twins have the exact same genetic material. They form in the mother when a fertilized egg splits into two embryos. Each embryo carries an exact copy of the genetic "building plan."

Plants often clone themselves. Aspen trees, for example, send out underground shoots. The shoots grow into new trees. The new trees have the same gene patterns as their parent tree.

Farmers take cuttings from trees that grow the biggest fruit. They replant the cuttings. The cuttings grow into new fruit trees. This practice increases the chances of getting good crops.

Many farmers wish they could use the same technique with animals. The difference is that animals breed through sexual reproduction. The mother provides the egg, which contains her genes. The male provides his genes through sperm. When the egg and sperm meet, the genes combine to create offspring. Some of the mother's traits are passed on, and some are left out. The same goes for the father's traits.

Debating Dolly

Since Dolly, many mammals have been cloned. The list includes goats, cows, pigs, cats, and dogs. Still, clones are expensive to produce. The process often fails.

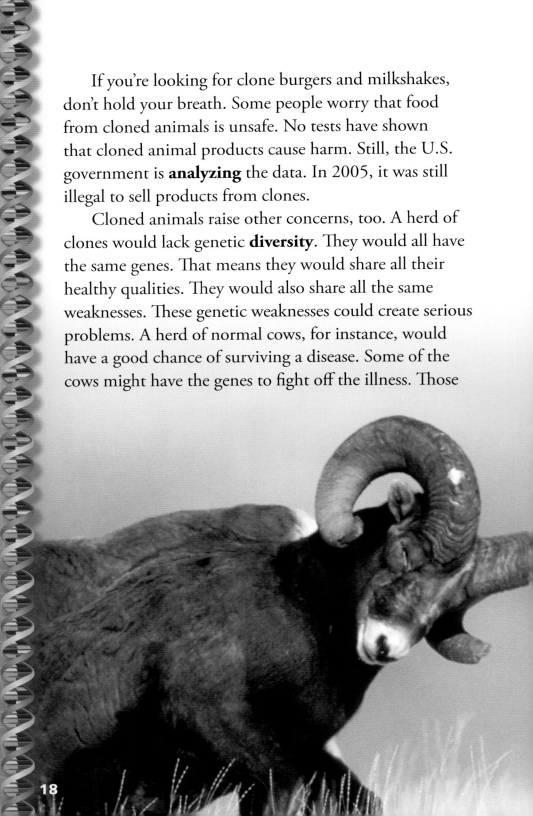

If you're looking for clone burgers and milkshakes, don't hold your breath. Some people worry that food from cloned animals is unsafe. No tests have shown that cloned animal products cause harm. Still, the U.S. government is **analyzing** the data. In 2005, it was still illegal to sell products from clones.

Cloned animals raise other concerns, too. A herd of clones would lack genetic **diversity**. They would all have the same genes. That means they would share all their healthy qualities. They would also share all the same weaknesses. These genetic weaknesses could create serious problems. A herd of normal cows, for instance, would have a good chance of surviving a disease. Some of the cows might have the genes to fight off the illness. Those cows would survive. A herd of clones, however, might lack the disease-fighting gene. The entire herd could be wiped out.

Individual clones may have health problems, too. No one has proven that Dolly got sick because she was a clone. Still, clones are created with genes from older animals. Their cells may behave as if they are older than they really are. Scientists are looking for a way around these health problems.

Cloning hasn't been around for long. We have a lot to learn about its effects. It offers many opportunities to scientists and farmers. It also **poses** many challenges. No one has yet cloned a human being. That day, however, may not be far away.

Genetic diversity helps a species survive.

Nature or Nurture?

A girl has brown eyes. She can speak English and Spanish. She has a nearly perfect ear for music. Which of these traits came from her genes? Which did she learn from the world around her?

This is the "Nature or Nurture" debate. Nature refers to traits that come from our genes. Nurture describes behaviors that we learn. Some people say our genes control most of who we are. Others say we learn our most important traits. Which side is right?

Most experts now agree that both sides contribute. Genes determine the color of your eyes. You learn English or Spanish from people around you. But what about skills like the ability to recognize musical notes? Here is where the question gets tricky.

Scientists at the University of California at San Francisco, did a study. They found that perfect pitch often runs in families. A grandfather, mother, and daughter might all have the ability to recognize musical notes. This suggests that the trait is genetic. Yet, the study also showed something else. Perfect pitch fades if a child does not study music by age six. This suggests that nurture also plays an important role in our development.

Researchers have found a similar pattern with some diseases. Emphysema, for example, can be caused by **defective** genes. Emphysema is a lung disease. It causes lung tissue to weaken. Normal genes produce a protein called AAt. AAt helps keep lung tissue healthy. When an AAt gene is damaged, the body doesn't produce enough of the protein.

Does that mean only people with that damaged gene need to worry about emphysema? No. Smoking damages lung tissue, too. Smokers are more likely than any other group of people to get emphysema—even if their genes are healthy.

Think of identical twins. They may look alike. They may have a lot in common. But they are unique individuals who make their own choices.

Genes can give you a good ear for music. Only practice will make someone a good musician.

ATTACK
OF THE
CLONES?

Are you afraid of clones? In the movie *Attack of the Clones*, thousands of clones are made from the cells of a fearsome warrior. Each clone has a single purpose in life. He obeys the orders of the evil emperor. Together, the clone army helps the emperor conquer the galaxy.

Is this the future of genetic engineering? Will robot-like clones take over Earth? No way, say the experts. First of all, cloning a human is not easy to do. We are not simple creatures. A lot could go wrong. Secondly, clones would not act like robots. They would be individuals. They would learn through their environment. They would have their own likes and dislikes. They would have the ability to choose. Finally, most people feel cloning humans is **unethical**. Many countries have made human cloning illegal.

Still, cloning human parts may be an exciting medical breakthrough that does a lot of good. Gene technology may completely transform the way doctors do their work.

The Fly **is a science-fiction movie about a scientist who transforms into a giant fly after an experiment goes wrong.**

New Blood

Cloning may lead to a medical revolution. Doctors know that cloning can produce complete organisms. Why couldn't it produce replacement parts?

If it could, many sick people would benefit. Here's one example. Leukemia is a serious blood cancer. It affects the bone marrow. Healthy bone marrow produces new blood cells.

One way to treat leukemia is with a bone marrow transplant. Yet, bone marrow is hard to transplant. The new marrow has to closely match the patient's marrow. Otherwise, the body destroys it.

What if doctors could grow healthy marrow from a patient's own cells? The match would be exact. The body would not reject the new marrow. Many lives might be saved in this way.

Some researchers are working with stem cells. These cells have a unique trait. They have not specialized, yet. They can grow into any type of cell the body needs. Doctors could mix stem cells with healthy cells from a patient's bone marrow. The stem cells would then grow into healthy marrow in the laboratory.

The problem is that stem cells come from human embryos. Some people feel that it is wrong to use embryos in this way. The debate is an important political issue. It may be up to your generation to decide. Think about it.

Mix and Match

Growing a cloned heart in a lab is problematic. Perhaps transplanting a pig's heart into a human being would be a better solution. That's exactly where transgenics may be leading. (Remember the spider-goat?) "There's no reason why the DNA of one species won't work in another species," explains Dr. Randy Lewis of the University of Wyoming. That's because genes are all made of the same chemicals.

Why would anyone want a pig's heart? Many patients die waiting for organ transplants. Using animal organs could save lives. Doctors have tried animal-to-human transplants. They've succeeded with heart valves from pigs. Transplanting whole organs has never worked. The human body rejects the animal organ.

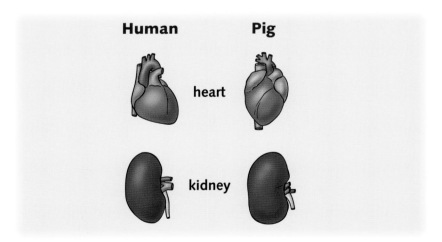

Pigs have some internal organs that are very similar to those of human beings.

Certain genes in animals cause humans to reject their organs. Pigs could possibly be engineered without those genes or with certain human genes. A patient's body might not **distinguish** between the pig and human heart.

Too Far, Too Fast?

Genetic research has opened up amazing scientific possibilities. It also raises tricky moral questions.

Scientists may soon be able to change genes in the womb. The procedure could correct genetic defects. Yet, what would keep parents from requesting "designer" genes? Some parents might choose only kids with certain features. What impact would that have on society?

Dr. Lewis thinks decisions like these are a long way off. "Our greatest fears are not possible," he says. Traits are stored in many different genes. Right now, scientists can't possibly locate them all.

Still, genetic scientists make discoveries every day. New ideas are already changing what we eat. New techniques are changing the way doctors treat patients. In your lifetime, you may see changes that are more amazing than an army of clones.

Transgenics may have many uses besides creating donor organs. For example, a human gene might be added to dairy cows. This could make milk easier for humans to digest. Some insects have special disease-fighting genes. Would you want your children to have a fly gene if it might save their lives?

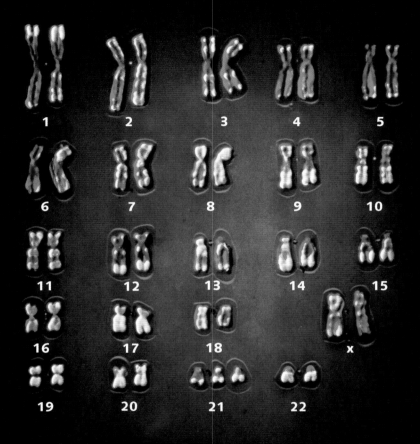

These are the chromosomes of a baby with Down Syndrome. Most people have 23 pairs of chromosomes. In people with Down Syndrome, the 21st pair has an extra chromosome.

Persuasive Essay: Why Human Cloning Is Wrong

by Matthew Eppinette

No one has yet cloned a human being. It may not be long before someone tries. Matthew Eppinette thinks that would be a huge mistake. He is Director of Research and Technology at The Center for Bioethics and Human Dignity in Illinois.

Cloning a person would be a terrible mistake. It is both dangerous and morally wrong. It will lower the value we place on human life.

Science has just begun to understand genetics and cloning. It will be years before we know the risks. Some cloned mice and other animals have had serious health problems. These include liver failure, **obesity**, and early death. Cloned babies might have the same problems.

Genetics may make the world a better place. But we must watch developments carefully. This is especially true when it comes to cloning and the modification of human genes.

Imagine a world where parents can pick and choose their kids' genes. Will having children someday be like ordering a car out of a catalog?

Will parents call their geneticist and say, "We want a boy with brown eyes. We want the extra-tall and extra-smart model?"

We must not turn the miracle of human life into a shopping trip. We must never let science turn people into products. Suppose people choose to clone themselves.

How alarming would that be? Would the clone be a person or property? If human clones are ever created, they must be treated with the same respect given to other people.

These are just some of the serious questions about cloning. We must think about them now. The day may soon come when science will force us to answer them.

Will human cloning be possible in your lifetime?

Glossary

alter (*verb*) to change

analyze (*verb*) to look closely at the facts in order to understand them

breakthrough (*noun*) a big step toward achieving a goal

cell (*noun*) a very small unit of life; all living things are made of cells

chromosome (*noun*) the part of a cell that contains genes

clone (*noun*) an exact genetic copy of a plant or animal

defective (*adjective*) having a fault or weakness

distinguish (*verb*) to tell the difference between one thing and another

diversity (*noun*) variety

gene (*noun*) the part of a cell that determines how a living thing looks and grows

genetic (*adjective*) having to do with genes, the units that determine how things will grow

genome (*noun*) the full set of chromosomes in a living thing

immune (*adjective*) protected against a disease

mammal (*noun*) a warm-blooded animal that has a backbone

microscopic (*adjective*) so small that it can only be seen with a microscope

modify (*verb*) to change

nucleus (*noun*) the central part of a cell that contains chromosomes

obesity (*noun*) the condition of being overweight

organism (*noun*) any living thing, such as a plant or animal

pesticide (*noun*) a poison designed to kill insects or other pests

pollination (*noun*) the passing of pollen from flower to flower in order to produce seeds

pose (*verb*) to present a question or problem

protein (*noun*) a chemical found in the cells of all living things

tinker (*verb*) to change or repair in an unskilled way

trait (*noun*) a special quality that makes one person or thing different from another

unethical (*adjective*) not consistent with the way people are supposed to behave; immoral

unique (*adjective*) not like anything else

vaccine (*noun*) a drug that helps protect the body against disease

Idioms

don't hold your breath (*page 18*) do not expect to get something
If you're waiting for cars that fly, don't hold your breath.

Index